Weidenfeld and Nicolson London

PANORAMAS
· OF ENGLISH GARDENS ·

TEXT BY DAVID WHEELER PHOTOGRAPHS BY NICK MEERS

Text © DAVID WHEELER, 1991
Photographs © NICK MEERS, 1991

First published in Great Britain by
Weidenfeld and Nicolson Ltd, 91 Clapham High Street, London SW4 7TA

Designed by NICK AVERY

British Library Cataloguing in Publication Data
Wheeler, David
  Panoramas of English gardens.
  1. England. Gardens
  I. Title   II. Meers, Nick 1955–
  712.60942
  ISBN 0–297–82085–6

Half-title page The oval pond, Easton Neston, Northamptonshire
Title page: Michaelmas daisies at the Old Court Nurseries, Worcestershire
Endpapers: Heathers at Holehird Gardens, Cumbria

CONTENTS

INTRODUCTION

The term 'English Garden' has become a label. It has taken on a meaning of excellence which is bandied about as far away from the shores of England as Japan, the United States of America and parts of Australasia. I have heard it used in hushed tones in rather the same way as some people refer to the manufacturer of their luggage or, worse, the designer of their T-shirts. It has put pressures upon an innocent phrase which, at times, it finds hard to carry.

On a recent lecture trip to America I was invited to see a number of 'English Gardens'. One, certainly, had the semblance and something like the 'feel' of an English garden; another was a bold attempt at copying a *particular* English garden; and the rest amounted to little more than a collection of pale-coloured perennials assembled together in a strip and 'marketed' as being pure

Surrey. On an earlier visit to America – in late winter – I saw other so-called 'English Gardens', which sadly looked no more like a garden than a collection of woody, half-living relics, wrapped up in hessian and the remains of Christmas tree branches to protect the poor plants from the sort of frosts England does not know. Fortunately there is at present among Americans a timely and strong recognition of their *own* gardening heritage, and I was happy to meet large numbers of people who are not slavishly following the paths pioneered by Gertrude Jekyll, William Robinson, Vita Sackville-West, *et al.*

It is worth looking at the parts of an 'English Garden' to see exactly what they contain. Let us take a typical herbaceous border – that uniquely English component – in, say, a Wiltshire garden. There are penstemons (from North America and Mexico),

PREVIOUS PAGE *The Queen's Garden at Sudeley Castle, Gloucestershire, with the ruins of the Banqueting Hall behind (see pp. 50–57).*

chrysanthemums (from China, Japan and Korea), delphiniums (from continental Europe, Asia and northern Africa), lupins, rudbeckias, golden rods and tobacco plants (from the Americas), and, when it comes to the multitude of bulbous species, we find ourselves directed to the floras of a hundred countries in several continents. In our same Wiltshire garden we will also find eucalyptus (from Australia), viburnums (from the Far East), cistuses (from all round the Mediterranean), and buddleias (from Chile and Peru).

Admittedly we grow a few native plants, and many which established themselves here so long ago that they are popularly thought to be of English origin. (The mulberry is a good example: all old English vicarage gardens are supposed to have one, and while they seem so much at home among our apple and nut trees, they came originally from China via southern Europe in the early seventeenth century to support English silk manufacturing.)

So an 'English Garden' is, in one light, a sort of botanical zoo for exotic plants from around the temperate world. It is how we have put them together that matters, not forgetting the all-important, generally benign English climate which allows these 'come-overs' to stand on our lawns and in our borders throughout English winters without the hessian wraps referred to earlier.

It is not only our plants that have come to us from across the seas; we have also borrowed gardening styles from other countries. How would our great formal gardens have developed if our designers had not visited France and Italy or if eminent garden-makers from those countries had not come to England?

Given the simply enormous range of plants that will adapt to England – Wales, Scotland and Ireland, too – it is not surprising that the idea of an 'English Garden' has travelled so far, nor is it surprising that people all round the world should want one for themselves. They sound easy, and it is only human nature to

want a little of what someone else has; hence, partly, the occurrance of Chinese or Japanese gardens, for instance, in Europe and North America.

In this book we bring together images of a number of English gardens which, in their diversity, are typical of the non-typical 'English Garden'. From the Cotswolds there are Misarden Park, Sudeley and Beverston Castles and Ewen Manor which, as one group alone, offer a rich and generous sample of English garden-making skills and practices. At Lime Kiln in Essex there are probably more roses than you are likely to find in any other private garden, anywhere. Not far away, at Beth Chatto's White Barn House, there is one of England's best collections of Mediterranean plants and a nursery devoted to their propagation. At David Hicks's garden, The Grove, in Oxfordshire there is res-

traint and the masterly use of space in unusual and imaginative ways. There is classicism and history at Hever Castle in Kent and at Easton Neston in Northamptonshire. At Flintham Hall in Nottinghamshire there is bountiful colour combined with stately parkland views. At Old Court Nurseries in Hereford and Worcester, within sight of the Malvern Hills, there is one of the finest collections of Michaelmas daisies, and at The Priory nearby there is a lovingly made garden with three superb borders well able to hold their own against the best in the land. Chatsworth is known to thousands of country house and garden visitors from around the world; here we see its maze from an unusual angle, and we can marvel at the engineering skills employed by Sir Joseph Paxton, just one of that garden's contributing landscapers. Still in the north of England we visit the outstanding

PREVIOUS PAGE *At Levens Hall, Cumbria, the topiary has just been clipped and will remain unchanged throughout the winter (see pp. 118–123).*

garden of York Gate made by Mrs Spencer and her late husband and son; and a few miles away, at Sutton-on-the-Forest, we look straight into the face of a beautiful formal house with finely dressed terraces. Also in Yorkshire is Old Sleningford Hall, a garden incorporating a large mill pond with four islands. In the Lake District we inspect the remarkable topiary at Levens Hall, and revel in the autumn colours at Holehird Gardens, which enjoys views over Lake Windermere. In the far south-west we glimpse spectacular camellias in the Cornish garden of Chyverton, which is also renowned for its mature magnolias; and in Hampshire we explore Jenkyn Place, one of England's great gardens, as it approaches its fiftieth birthday.

Several of these gardens are extremely well known, others less so, one or two hardly at all. What they all share now is a set of remarkable photographs taken by Nick Meers with his panoramic camera.

When I was first told what this extraordinary camera could do I felt a mixture of excitement and apprehension. (I imagined wide-angle photographs with their distorted verticals.) A few weeks later, on a separate assignment unrelated to this book, I met Nick Meers in the garden at Snowshill Manor in Gloucestershire. Nick began to explain what his camera could do (crudely speaking, wide angles *without* distortion) and I became more enthusiastic. A beer table may be no place to examine a photographer's portfolio but at an early suggestion we retired for lunch in the village pub, and after we had disposed of our ploughman's platters I was shown examples of colour transparencies – held up to the pub windows – which I recall to this day as making me tingle with pleasure.

I had not imagined how much landscape or garden could be brought into one viewfinder, and I was amazed at how the tripod could be positioned so that images other than straight-on views

could be made. I am not a photographer in any professional sense of the word, so I soon became lost in the jargon of camera-speak. Nick, I think, realized my technical bewilderment and allowed his portfolio to do the talking.

Eagerly we began to compile a provisional list of gardens – much depended on the time we would have, and on the sort of summer ahead of us. Before we could get ourselves into gear we had lost certain opportunities. But we had a long list to draw on (there are well over 2400 gardens open to the public in England) so it was to be a matter of careful choosing. As the summer progressed I talked on the telephone to Nick at his London flat from my home in Wales. Fortunately he is a man who is prepared to make early starts and linger into the evening to catch those two fabled times of day when photographers often do their best work. There was a drought in the summer of 1990 and almost no work could be done in August or early September because plants failed and lawns turned brown as a result of hosepipe watering restrictions. But shorter days and heavy dews revived many gardens by October, although it was not a vintage year for autumn colour – many trees had defoliated because of the shortage of moisture.

Much later in the year we met to look at the transparencies on a light box. Then began the long and difficult task of selecting those photographs which recorded the best aspects of Nick's endeavours.

The results are contained within the covers of this book. The chosen photographs are not meant to represent the 'English Garden' in all its manifestations – that would require many volumes

PREVIOUS PAGE *Afternoon sun falls on Beverston Castle in the Cotswolds. Shade is cast by the keep of the 13th-century ruin (see pp. 30–35).*

and all the seasons several times round. What we *have* assembled is a personal choice which we hope conveys both the *spirit* of

English Gardens and a taste of their curious and delightful compositions.

Note
Details of the opening times and locations of most gardens in this book can normally be found in the 'Yellow Book', *Gardens of England & Wales*, published annually by the National Gardens

Scheme, but please note that The Grove and Lime Kiln are not open to the public.

FOLLOWING PAGE *The double herbaceous borders at Jenkyn Place in Hampshire in their midsummer glory, protected by yew walls (see pp. 70–79).*

THE GARDENS

White Barn House

ELMSTEAD MARKET, ESSEX

Beth Chatto's name is synonymous with unusual plants. She grows them – hardy perennials mostly – in huge numbers and propagates many of them to sell in her nursery. Her catalogue, like the practical and important books she has written, belongs in every gardener's library. Mrs Chatto began work at White Barn thirty years ago, and today her garden ranks with Rosemary Verey's Barnsley House in Gloucestershire as one of the two privately owned English gardens most familiar to today's green-fingered *cognoscenti*. Her celebrated gardening career began as a flower arranger and lecturer under the influence of a former neighbour, Mrs Desmond Underwood, who in her own right earned a permanent niche in the horticultural hall of fame for her book about silver-foliage plants. Beth Chatto's other mentor was the painter Sir Cedric Morris, whose nearby Benton End was a plantsman's Mecca in the 1950s and 60s. The garden at White Barn House today takes in twenty acres. There is a Mediterranean Garden where low growing, often pungent-leaved natives of the *maquis* feel very much at home on dry Essex gravel, and there is a series of ponds whose waterside planting from early spring to late summer is spectacular. Herbaceous perennials occupy great areas of vast curving beds where bulbs, occasional annuals and biennials cover the ground thickly between shrubs and trees. There is no formality at White Barn House (except of course the immaculately kept stockbeds and plant sales area), and those people seeking precision-clipped yew and box must go elsewhere. This is a riotous garden, grand and luxuriant in its planting and comparatively straightforward in its upkeep.

Planting in the Chatto style: boldly contrasting leaf forms set against a palette that is not shy of strong colour.

White Barn House

By damming a stream running through her garden, Beth Chatto has created a series of connected ponds where she is able to indulge herself with a wide variety of plants that would not otherwise adapt to the garden's free-draining, gravelly soil. The crowns of *Gunnera manicata* must be protected in hard winters but in other respects the plant is undemanding, producing large tropical-looking leaves appropriate for waterside schemes. Peltiphyllum (now *Darmera peltata*) also has large flat leaves, with the added bonus of good autumn colour. Astilbes and hostas are always grateful for damp conditions but they are often found in conventional borders which do not suffer drought. These irises like water, too. Alchemilla is allowed to tumble over edges to mask any unnatural-looking lines.

Previous page

Beth Chatto's Mediterranean Garden lies either side of gravelled steps. It is so positioned as to catch every scrap of wayward sunshine in an attempt to imitate the dry and impoverished terrain so vital to the survival of plants which, while surprisingly tolerant of low temperatures in many cases, cannot put up with wet feet. Magenta-pink everlasting peas (*Lathyrus latifolius*) cushion the edge of the right-hand beds. On the left, tall daisy-like flowers bloom over long months. Verbascums, ghostly spikes of felt with slowly unfolding sulphur-yellow flowers, steely-blue thistles and soft ballota are typical of the flora dotted about southern Europe and ensnared now among the unlikely slopes of a garden within an hour's drive of London.

White Barn House

Here is more waterside planting, which also shows the way Mrs Chatto has treated the natural lie of the land at White Barn House. Mature trees not only cast welcome shade, they add scale and interest by stopping short the view and obscuring other parts of the garden from immediate sight. Clear yellow day-lilies and orange and orangey-red Asian candelabra primulas associate well with sky-blue forget-me-nots sprinkled along the entire length of the border. A bright patch of white arums reflects in the still water and more touches of white emanate from randomly seeded fox-gloves. Several grasses have also been used in this scheme and it is interesting now to note the widespread appeal of these hitherto largely neglected plants in English gardens.

Following page

Beth Chatto is also a nurserywoman. A visit to White Barn House offers a chance to buy that elusive plant whose name may have been preserved for months or years on a vital scrap of paper. The sales area, divided neatly into well-labelled sections, is supplied by the large field of stockbeds in which seed-raised or divided plants are left to grow on to provide ample propagating material. But these stockbeds are beautiful as well as practical. In blocks of pure pigment they appear to have been laid down rather as an abstract painter or Caucasian weaver might have arranged his colours. Here drifts of flat-topped yarrow, white and red thrifts, pearly artemisias and pink and blue veronicas lie randomly in tight rectangles like the ordered beds of an early physic garden.

Beverston Castle

BEVERSTON, GLOUCESTERSHIRE

Beverston Castle, a few miles west of Tetbury on the southern Cotswold plain, has one of England's most romantic garden settings. The thirteenth-century castle keep towers above the neighbouring church; the Cotswold-stone outbuildings and barns huddle around the seventeenth-century house which occupies the site of the castle's former banqueting chamber. Its terrace – linked to the garden by a bridge over a dry moat – is wide, long and south-facing; the cracks between the slabs are richly spangled with low-growing herbaceous plants and small shrubs. During the summer it is almost impossible to step between the crowded flowers, which flaunt themselves and obliterate the stone like a living carpet. On the wall of the house there are roses, *Magnolia grandiflora*, and ceanothus, the Californian lilac which revels in warmth and shelter. The dry moat is curtained with *Vitis coignetiae* falling into pools of irises below. The large lawn is studded with old and interesting trees. In springtime, paths are cut through the grass between clumps of naturalized narcissi. Flowering cherries carry the colour above head height in the early months. The large Kitchen Garden, surrounded by a high wall with fan-trained fruit, is divided into traditional allotment-like beds, not the fussy, more labour-intensive pattern of narrow beds in the French *potager* style. Vegetables share the space with rows of cutting flowers or plants like polyanthus, bedded out here for the summer period to renew their vigour for the following spring. At Beverston Mrs Rook has ensured a year-round cavalcade of colour and horticultural interest blended perfectly with ancient trees, old stone and mellow paving.

Afternoon sunshine highlights golden-leaved robinia in a long border of roses and herbaceous perennials backed by a low wall.

Beverston Castle

The keep of the thirteenth-century ruined castle dominates the western end of the house. Further 'battlements' of old English yew balance the picture and protect the terrace from biting east winds. In the walls of the dry moat red valerian seeds itself about freely. Spreading junipers flank the bridge which links the terrace to the rest of the garden. The old tree in the left foreground, a walnut thought to be well over two hundred years old, has fallen since this photograph was taken in July 1990. This photograph and caption are therefore something of a memorial and an obituary for a tree whose death is much mourned. Fortunately another old walnut survives near the gatehouse at Beverston Castle.

Following page

Rosa 'Mermaid' relishes the warmth on the south-facing wall overlooking the terrace at Beverston Castle. Euphorbias, with their lime-green bracts, billow beneath the windows. In cracks between the Cotswold-stone paving slabs there is a colourful assortment of summer-flowering plants which include dwarf campanulas, *Alchemilla mollis* (to echo the green of the euphorbias) and pink-flowered, ground-hugging thymes which release 'southern' aromatic fragrances on the still air. Valuable ever-grey foliage of stachys and senecio helps to balance the brighter colours regardless of whether the terrace is in sun or shade. A large clump of irises in the dry moat will have flowered earlier in the year and the rampant vine will display its rich, velvety russet and burgundy colours when the evenings begin to draw in.

Lime Kiln

CLAYDON, SUFFOLK

Humphrey Brooke, who made this garden, died on Christmas Eve, 1988. He was a man of many parts – in 1952 he was appointed secretary of the Royal Academy, and his interests ranged from Yorkshire cricket to politics and Victorian painting – but perhaps above all he was a rose fanatic. He grew them up and over his house, he let them invade his trees until their girth just above ground level made you wonder if the tree had been planted to grow up the rose; they had *carte blanche* to choke his pillared courtyard and in June and July you could almost find your way to his garden by following your nose from the centre of Claydon. Lime Kiln, a red-brick Tudor farmhouse, once belonged to Humphrey Brooke's grandmother-in-law, Countess Sophie Benckendorff, whose husband was the last Tsar's am-bassador in England. (When Mr Brooke once found a rose he could not identify he named it 'Sophie's Perpetual' in memory of his wife's grandmother, although rosarian Michael Gibson thinks it is the same plant as 'Dresden China' – such are the similarities between some roses and such is the mystery of their names.) The garden was neglected for several decades and no real work was done again until Mr and Mrs Brooke bought what might be called 'the old family home' in 1954. Trees planted by Countess Benckendorff in the 1880s still existed. The old rose garden was restored and many new roses acquired – some from the famous East German rose garden, Sangerhausen; others from friends and nurserymen all over Britain.

The archway in the brick wall leading to the pillared courtyard at Lime Kiln is festooned with climbing roses.

Lime Kiln

The roses at Lime Kiln grow everywhere. They weave their way into every tree and attempt to swamp the house, they lie prostrate over grass paths and hang in swags from the open doors of barns and outbuildings. Humphrey Brooke grew them in pots, too, changing all the soil after three or four years. There are thought to be over five hundred species and cultivars at Lime Kiln. Most can be described as Old Roses although some, bred in the past few decades, have the appearance of older varieties. With such a collection it is not surprising to learn that roses can be seen in flower from late spring until well into winter when some of the Chinas still produce a few blooms. Some roses in the garden remain unidentified. The real wonder of Lime Kiln is that the chalky soil is not considered to be right for roses!

Previous page
Here in the courtyard at Lime Kiln Humphrey Brooke allowed his roses to behave as they might in the wilder parts of his garden. Secateurs were only used to remove the most obstructing canes and branches. Dead-heading was not an important ritual in this garden; it is probably fair to say that Mr Brooke achieved his exuberant, riotous effects by breaking most gardeners' rules. Compare this romantic tangle of scented flowers and foliage to the often sterile and bleak-looking beds of roses found in some private gardens and municipal beds planted by local authorities. Beneath the roses there is a jungle of underplanting consisting of hardy geraniums, some day-lilies and drifts of wild cow parsley.

Misarden Park

MISERDEN, GLOUCESTERSHIRE

Misarden Park occupies one of those remote, deeply cleft Cotswold valleys where the house seems to sail over its own landscape. The main part of the building dates from 1620; the grandfather of the present owner, Major Wills, bought the property in 1914, commissioning Edwin Lutyens to remodel the east wing after a fire five years later. Lutyens also possibly influenced the reconstruction of the garden, which in the seventeenth century, according to an existing engraving by Kip, was very formal indeed. Today the garden layout is much simpler although there are formal elements, like the magnificent pair of three-hundred-foot-long herbaceous borders between which visitors these days enter. Near to the house is a pair of much smaller borders, where silver-leaved plants, spilling over a wall, blend happily with the grey stone. A border in front of the house, running for forty yards or so, is edged in catmint, whose blue summer-long haze is the perfect foil for buddleias and pale pink roses. There are fine trees at Misarden and an arboretum stands today where in the 1920s many hands toiled over a rock garden of huge proportions. Weeping elm, black walnut, mulberry, purple beech and liquidambar can be numbered among the rarer specimens, including the Indian bean tree (*Catalpa bignonioides*) and *Davidia involucrata*, the pocket-handkerchief tree. A newly planted rose garden brings together some of the best modern Hybrid Teas and a collection of roses bred in Victorian times. In places rough grass is allowed where wild flowers are colonizing. This is one of England's lesser-known gardens, able now to stand comparison with many old favourites.

Catmint edges the border in front of the terrace, while steps cut in grass are decorated with blue and white alyssum.

Misarden Park

The pair of herbaceous borders at Misarden Park is among the largest in the country. Each is some three hundred feet long by thirty feet broad. On the far side one is backed by a high yew hedge topped with domed castellations, forming one side of a yew walk separating the borders from the rose garden and kitchen garden. At an approximate half-way point the borders are traversed by a path which cuts through the yew walk leading to the kitchen garden one way, and to the cedar walk the other. Pergolas made of rustic wooden poles form canopies over the path, their roses adding to midsummer's riot of colour. On the pergolas seen here there are 'Goldfinch', a rose with a rich fruity fragrance bred in Edwardian times, the ever-popular 'Albertine' bred in France soon after the First World War, and 'Paul's Himalayan Musk', whose parentage is unknown. The borders run roughly east to west; there are many peonies, and plenty of hardy geraniums, irises, poppies, tall stands of macleaya (the plume poppy), low-growing pinks, and alchemilla whose acid yellowy-green, long-lasting flowers help other colours to achieve their required degree of prominence.

Misarden Park

There are many delightfully contrasting
garden areas at Misarden Park; here mown
grass meets meadow. The hedge of 'Felicia'
roses divides the smooth from the rough.
Wild flowers have established themselves in
the long grass and they are allowed to seed
themselves before the grass is cropped. More
roses have been planted in the wilder part as
companions for cherry trees, mountain ash,
golden yew and other trees. 'Felicia' is an
English-bred Hybrid Musk rose raised in
1928. Often recommended for specimen
planting, it adapts well to this kind of
scheme. Its flowers are freely borne
throughout summer and autumn and they
have a strong aromatic fragrance. Beneath
the roses here there is a collection of old-
fashioned pinks.

Previous page
Tall blocks of clipped yew stand sentinel-like
at the brim of the wide south-west-facing
terrace. A border runs the full length of the
house. *Buddleia* 'Lochinch', with silvery
leaves and stems and fragrant lilac-blue
flowers in late summer, and bushes of
'Penelope' rose form a backdrop to dark-blue
delphiniums and the magnificent thick
ribbon of catmint which throws its gauzy,
blue-flowering stems all summer long. At the
far end of the terrace there is a mist of
Crambe cordifolia and white rosebay willow
herb, *Epilobium angustifolium* 'Album'. The
cedar of Lebanon, with branches right to the
ground, has been lucky to escape the storm
damage suffered by so many large forest trees
in English gardens in recent years.

Sudeley Castle

WINCHCOMBE, GLOUCESTERSHIRE

Over three hundred years ago when Henry VIII's last queen, Catherine Parr, lived at Sudeley Castle, she would have looked out onto Cotswold countryside which probably appeared much the same to her eyes as it does to ours today. Earlier still Richard III would have surveyed the same scene when he owned the castle. Today the ruins are laced with climbing roses allowed to hang in swags like fragrant curtains. Fine gravel walks divide the formal garden where herbs and more roses bring order and sweet smells to a patterned garden whose design, if not construction, is as old as the sixteenth-century queen. In recent years the gardens have been remade by Jane Fearnley-Whittingstall working with Lady Ashcombe. In 1989 thousands of visitors to London's Chelsea Flower Show were treated to a glimpse of Sudeley's ethereal qualities when Mrs Fearnley-Whittingstall threaded delicate-looking roses through pieces of Sudeley's honey-coloured masonry in an award-winning display. While the Chelsea exhibit lasted for less than a week, the real Sudeley is there all the year, and visitors from around the world come to enjoy its bowery walkways and secret places during the long summer months. Apart from the famed Queen's Garden there are other gardens within gardens, which may surprise those people who expect to find only formality. The Mulberry Garden is a small area shaded by a now much-layered tree from which the plot takes its name. Early in the year there will be rich tapestry colours from inky hellebores and bright crown imperials. Later they will be followed by peonies and day-lilies. In an adjoining courtyard, roses are sold from an excellent long list, which includes many unusual varieties and rarely encountered species.

Blue sky can be seen through the ruined tracery of the Banqueting Hall windows, where, inside, roses hang like curtains on the exposed walls.

Sudeley Castle

In the Queen's Garden and Tudor Herb
Garden there is a pool which sends up a fine
jet of water. Surrounded by stone
balustrading, it makes the perfect
centrepiece. Pale and dark lavender and
purple sage are grown in segments
surrounding stone urns. Other beds are filled
with a mixture of herbs and herbaceous
perennials among the roses to ensure a
prolonged flowering season. Among the rose
varieties here are shell-pink 'New Dawn',
'Albéric Barbier' with glossy foliage and
creamy-yellow buds and flowers, and
'Félicité et Perpétue', a magnificent cultivar
named in 1827 after the two daughters of its
French breeder, M. Jacques, who in turn
were named after two Christian martyrs
who died in the early years of the second
century AD.

Previous page
A view of part of the Queen's Garden and
Tudor Herb Garden seen from the church
tower. The geometric pattern of beds is a
long-established garden layout. Similar ideas
based on medieval designs can be found in
gardens around the world. Sometimes they
appear without any flowering-plant
embellishment; in other instances, like the
French *jardin potager*, they will be filled with
vegetables. Here the paths are of grass and
gravel allowing easy access to all the beds.
The surrounding yew hedges provide both
shelter and privacy. Rose frames have been
fashioned from metal and are surmounted by
a simple metalwork crown. The flight of
steps on the left hand side leads to a raised
terrace on the east side.

Following page
This encompassing view incorporates the ruins of the Banqueting Hall and parts of the Castle used today for craft workshops, restaurant and a permanent exhibition of lace and needlework. Hidden from view is a nursery offering a spectacular range of old and unusual rose varieties. On the right is the Chapel (St Mary's Church) whose parapet overlooks the Queen's Garden and Tudor Herb Garden. The broad flat-topped hedges surround the intricate pattern of herb-edged beds where, in summer, sweet scents rise from the mixture of aromatic plants and fragrant roses. Tall domes of clipped yews appear to add their own architectural element to the structure which remains solid throughout the year and act as guardians of the temporary pageant of colour issuing from the well-filled beds and borders. The walkways around the hedges lead to terraces at various levels from which it is possible either to reflect upon the drama of the Castle and its attendant buildings or to relax on a bench where far-reaching views of the Cotswold hills exercise their calming influence.

Old Sleningford Hall

RIPON, YORKSHIRE

Old Sleningford Hall dates from 1810. Its garden is on two levels: extensive lawns around the domestic buildings, and hedges and borders beside a large mill pond, which once fed the flour mill wheel. Among the many trees near the house is an old copper beech whose lower branches have layered themselves in a circle around the main trunk which, because of gales, has been cropped to a forty-foot stump. The Rt Hon. James and Mrs Ramsden have been making their garden for the last thirty-five years. For a backdrop they have the old mill, now covered with wisteria, and brick walls, which run along two sides of the Kitchen Garden. Of four islands on the mill pond, only one is reached by a bridge. A lawn mower is transported by boat to another island where the grass is cut during the summer months.

Juliet Ramsden grows many plants whose flowers and foliage dry well for winter decoration. In her borders can be found clumps of fennel, lavender, achillea, poppies, echinops and centaureas as well as the more familiar 'drying flowers' like helichrysums and stachys. Tall spikes of mullein also dry well, as do the heads of giant hogweed (*Heracleum mantegazzianum*). Honesty grows in profusion, but here it is picked when the seed pods are still green, thus offering an alternative to the usually encountered beige, and by picking them before they ripen some control is maintained over riotous self-seeding. Many of the dried flowers can be bought on days when the garden opens to the public.

A long herbaceous border seen across the mill pond at Old Sleningford Hall.

Old Sleningford Hall

There are no formal gardens at Old Sleningford. Trees and shrubs have been arranged to form a close-knit fabric of seemingly impenetrable foliage. From time to time there has to be some hacking back of invasive limbs, and undergrowth has to be cleared to prevent all the plants becoming choked. In this waterside environment trees and shrubs are rarely inhibited by periods of drought which can so drastically affect other parts of the garden. The first autumn leaves have begun to fall. Soon the island (on the left) will seem bare, but within two or three months the first snowdrops will bloom. These will be followed later by daffodils and anemones whose flowers will enjoy the warming sunshine before the leafy canopy once more obscures the summer skies.

Following page

The early-morning mist begins to clear, revealing the almost surreal image of Mercury, who appears for a moment to light upon the still water. In reality he is a permanent fixture poised upon a ball but here, reflected in the proverbially calm mill pond, he becomes a possession of the sky above. Secondary images of autumn colour from birches, beeches and ornamental acers also glow on the mirrored surface. The octagonal summer-house sits on the one island which can be reached by a narrow bridge. Pampas grass grows among the trees, and in the spring the grass is spangled with colourful bulbs. The water depth varies between eight and ten feet, and twice in the past thirty-five years the Ramsdens have had to clear it of silt washed into the pond by the stream which feeds it.

Easton Neston

TOWCESTER, NORTHAMPTONSHIRE

Easton Neston was built by Nicholas Hawksmoor and completed in 1702 for Sir William Fermor, later Lord Lempster. Previous writers have noted similarities between its façade and that of Louis XV's Petit Trianon, although Easton Neston predates that famous French pavilion by half a century. Writing in 1978, Nigel Nicolson described the house as 'a palace in miniature', built of Helmdon stone, 'unmottled, and unveined, as clear as liquid, but where it is rounded, as in the two vast columns on either side of the front door, it acquires a certain swarthiness, like a lion's pelt'. He goes on to say that the Corinthian capitals 'are as sharp as freshly cut acanthus leaves'. The gateposts frame a view of Greens Norton church two miles away. Lord Hesketh laid out the present garden installing a large oval pond which beautifully reflects the garden front of the house with its high windows and roof-top balustrading. The topiary yews, fashioned like embroidery work, which can be seen today, were also planted by Lord Hesketh. More topiary, made of box this time, is situated on the terrace overlooking the oval pond. Pieces of statuary came from Stowe when the Duke of Buckingham sold his estate in 1923. The arboretum, with its fine collection of mostly coniferous trees, dates from this period, too. There is also a large walled garden with an avenue of espaliered apple trees and a new west-facing border. Most of the roses at Easton Neston are old-fashioned varieties, including many climbers on the wall which runs from the house to the oval pond.

Curling yew topiary hedges at Easton Neston, with autumn colour beginning to appear in the arboretum.

Easton Neston

A magnificent view stretches across the oval pond, between the evergreen portal of sombre conifers to a distant formal canal, itself flanked by a double avenue of trees; the eye is drawn inexorably to the wooded horizon. Crisply cut hedges embrace the pool in two sweeping planes of topiary as flawless as their reflection. Classical statues punctuate these 'living walls' at regular intervals: the carved stone figures survey the watery arena and each other with equal impassivity. Here there is calm, here there is order, here there is logic. Even the *broderie* spiral hedges, resembling snails, complement the pedestal drums of yew which rise from the terrace and stand happily to attention on this serene yet none the less powerful parade-ground.

Pages 66–7

Easton Neston's formal façade reflected in the still waters of the oval pond on a cold March day. The treescape of deciduous and coniferous trees (including a tall cedar of Lebanon) is boldly outlined by the wintery light, which appears to illuminate the skeletal forms of the mature deciduous specimens from within. The boy rides his dolphin; the spouting water causes only the minimum of ripples on the surface of the water. The formal terrace could be a landing stage for a mythical barge which might appear at any moment: this is classical allusion convincingly portrayed.

Jenkyn Place

BENTLEY, HAMPSHIRE

Jenkyn Place occupies a gradually sloping site in the north-east corner of Hampshire near the Surrey town of Farnham. The village of Bentley (where Lord Baden-Powell lived at Pax Hill) stretches along the Guildford-to-Winchester road beside the River Wey. From the garden at Jenkyn Place there are views across to Alice Holt Forest. Mr and Mrs Coke came here in 1941 but obligations to the war effort prevented any immediate attempt at making a garden until peace was restored. The intervening years served as a useful lesson in becoming acquainted with the land so that when the time arrived to put plans into action the Cokes had already abandoned first ideas. The remains of an earlier garden could be detected and use was made of existing yew hedges. More hedges were planted and they play an important role in this 'compartmented' garden. They form long vistas, enclose courtyards and provide visually impenetrable backdrops to herbaceous borders. Garden walls and old farm buildings have been clothed with roses and other climbers whose fragrances are exaggerated by and trapped in sunny corners. Separate 'rooms' are devoted to different themes. In the Sundial Garden terracotta pots filled with geraniums stand on the paving in summer. This is a large garden, in the grand manner. Apart from the intimate enclosures there are vast sweeps of lawn and areas where specimen trees stand about in longer grass. Gerald Coke died in 1990 having been fortunate enough to realize many of his gardening ambitions. His widow carries on, and their son John runs a nursery full of interesting and unusual plants just a few minutes' drive away.

In this 'room', enclosed by walls of yew, a sundial stands surrounded, throughout the summer months, by pots of pelargoniums.

Jenkyn Place

The Herb Garden at Jenkyn Place is arranged around a raised disc of grey stone flags between whose cracks seedlings have taken firm root. Many herbs and other aromatic plants enjoy dry conditions such as these. On warm days the heat is absorbed by the stone and given back on long evenings when the various scents and aromas are at their strongest – particularly after a light shower of summer rain. Scattered here around a statue of Bacchus with his cup and significant bunch of grapes are fennel, hyssop, mint, various sages, French tarragon, chives, button-flowered double feverfew, pale lavender and green santolina whose flowers are a better shade of yellow than most of the grey-leaved varieties. Surrounding the herbs is a circle of apple trees trained on posts and wire, with roses and honeysuckles at their feet.

Previous page

The long pair of herbaceous borders at Jenkyn Place is divided by a grass path. The north border is backed by a long yew hedge, while on the south side the hedge is of box. Stone slabs have been laid as a margin to the path to take the wear of many pairs of visiting feet. Gertrude Jekyll, who lived at Munstead Wood near Godalming, a dozen or so miles away, would have admired both the scale and content of these borders. Although not graded in the classic Jekyll manner, they do embrace many of the colours which she chose for her own schemes sixty and more years ago. Brick gate piers topped with stone urn finials bring the borders to an elegant full stop. The shrubby mallow, with a silvery sheen to its magenta flowers, occurs in the top right of this picture and at the far end of the border.

Jenkyn Place

At Jenkyn Place there are a number of enclosures made either of yew and box hedges or by runs of old walling surrounding the elegant red-brick house. This archway reveals an inner courtyard containing a lead tub filled with tender daturas. On the wall is a pink rose with glossy foliage. This specimen was discovered here after Mr and Mrs Coke's arrival in the 1940s. No one, it seems, can identify it accurately, which reminds us how very similar in form, and in flower shape, many roses are. Roses are among the best documented plants in horticultural libraries, yet many of the authorities have pinned several names to one plant. A further modern-day dilemma occurs when plants ordered from a nursery arrive without their label or, as sometimes happens, are wrongly named.

Pages 76–7

Mallows (*Lavatera olbia* 'Rosea') act as bookends to the north-facing herbaceous border. At the far end an evergreen apse of clipped yew shelters a semi-circular stone seat. The border planting is close, the colours are rich. Day-lilies and hardy herbaceous geraniums stand well with lime-green alchemilla. Dark blue anchusa, delphiniums and lavender are softened by grey-leaved stachys; pinks and white violas fill in along the edges, and taller perennials in shades of white and yellow stand out well against the dark green hedges. A brick path crosses the grass path on its narrow journey from the Sundial Garden. From this (eastern) end of the border another vista opens up to reveal a gazebo across the grass some distance away.

Ewen Manor

EWEN, GLOUCESTERSHIRE

Ewen Manor once stood on the opposite bank of the Thames to the one it stands on now. It was moved, stone by stone, two hundred years ago. When Colonel and Mrs Gibbs came here in the mid-1940s they made a large sunken rose garden in an area which had been devoted to wartime 'Dig for Victory' potato production. In turn the rose garden has been transformed again; it has now become a grassed area with corner beds, each a home for a small statue among shrubs and perennial flowers. Shade is cast by an old, spreading cedar of Lebanon which despite its great age continues to stand against the onslaught of furious, present-day storms. A long border of herbaceous plants and small shrubs runs on a gentle slope at right angles to the house. It is faced by a row of eleven golden yew 'puddings', similar to those which HRH The Prince of Wales inherited at Highgrove

House not far away. Tree peonies and roses are this border's mainstays, while through the seasons a changing cavalcade of rich-coloured flowers makes its appearance. Throughout Cotswold gardens there can be found unusual garden buildings made from local stone. At Ewen Manor we find a round open-fronted summer-house with a conical roof of stone tiles. In an enclosed garden bounded by yew hedges and converted stables Mrs Gibbs has placed a rectangular stone-edged pool where water-lily flowers and leaves almost obscure the water's surface in high summer. The surrounding pavement is encrusted with jewel-like helianthemums and *Dianthus* species, which in turn are surrounded by freely seeded *Alchemilla mollis* bringing acid yellows to the galaxy of other colours.

Dark yew hedges and closely cut grass surround the pool like a frame and mount in a perfectly assembled picture.

Ewen Manor

Clipped golden yews line the edge of the grass path running along the mixed border. The yellow- and red-flowered tree peonies have finished blooming but their distinctive foliage remains all summer long as a foil for the herbaceous plants whose moments of glory may be brief or prolonged. Beneath the tree peony here is a patch of *Alstroemeria* Ligtu Hybrids, whose narrow colour range includes shades of coral and milky-orange. Poppies associate well with the rich colour of the lax shrub rose spilling its spent petals on the grass. Touches of yellow come from day-lilies and the flat heads of achillea. Dark blue anchusa – a member of the borage family – adds strong accents of colour while a six-foot-high cloud of *Crambe cordifolia* sails over its neighbours. At the far end of the vista created by the border and line of yews there is a fine specimen of *Cytisus battandieri*, the Moroccan broom, with bright yellow pineapple-scented flowers among a mass of silver-backed leaves.

Previous page
This grand view across the garden at Ewen Manor encompasses a sundial on the warm terrace and the clipped golden yews standing proudly against the long herbaceous border. The backdrop is formed by a high hedge of dark green yew and towering trees which stand in the furthest reaches of the garden. Roses and sun-loving shrubs like cistuses are set about the paving while larger plants have been allowed to roll over the stone retaining-walls, which drop a few feet to the lower, grassed level. The components of this scene have been cleverly put together so that from any standpoint in the garden there is a magnificent view, which, particularly here in summer, looks crowded, yet peaceful and serene.

Flintham Hall

NR NEWARK, NOTTINGHAMSHIRE

Members of one family have lived at Flintham Hall for over two hundred years. Myles Thoroton Hildyard can look out of his windows today and enjoy views of parkland planted by his ancestors. Lebanon cedars, Turkey oak (*Quercus cerris*) and *Quercus × hispanica* 'Lucombeana' (the Lucomb oak, a variety raised by an Exeter nurseryman in 1762) are among distinguished and sometimes rare examples of specimen trees on the estate. In the mid-1850s Thomas Thoroton Hildyard, Member of Parliament for South Nottinghamshire, engaged local architect T. C. Hine to remodel the house and at the same time he added the magnificent structure which has been described as 'the most remarkable nineteenth-century conservatory in the whole of England'. It is made of glass on a stone framework with a glass and ironwork dome reaching above the roofline of the house. The great height of the conservatory was calculated so that palms could be grown. Nowadays, with roof-threatening palms long gone, the building houses a 'tamer' variety of specimens including daturas, abutilon, begonias, mimosa which flowers early in the year, and tree ferns from New Zealand that would perish in this part of England without the protection of glass. Mr Hine also built the wide terrace on the south side of the house, with steps leading down to the garden in the centre and at both ends. With only one gardener Myles Hildyard maintains the five-acre garden within forty acres of a park to a very high standard. Although some five thousand annuals are reared for bedding out each year, the garden is rich in permanent plants including many roses.

Flintham Hall, seen in July from over a colourful corner of the garden. Flower-filled urns decorate the formal terrace.

Flintham Hall

Low box hedges define the boundaries of these flower borders. A seated figure, made of lead, watches over the scene. *Clematis* 'Ville de Lyon' scrambles into a neighbouring rose. The irises have been succeeded by fragrant tobacco plants, pom-pom dahlias, a few poppies, rudbeckias and penstemons. Borders like these can be filled with a wide assortment of annual and perennial flowering plants. They can be colour-graded to include just a few shades, or they can reflect the more carefree abundance of cottage-garden flowers. Bulbs can be planted to bring in early colour and as their foliage begins to die back the summer plants will mask the debris and maintain the colourful effect.

Previous page

Peaches ripen slowly on the red brick wall, which acts as the backdrop to a border whose front edge is contained by a low box hedge. The planting here consists of verbascums, whose yellow flowering spikes emerge from a tight rosette of grey felt-like leaves, hollyhocks in shades of pale yellow and rosy pink, bush roses, striped grass and a patch of sweet-scented tobacco plants in pale pink and white. Running through these plants are stands of the giant Scotch or cotton thistle, *Onopordum acanthium*, which can reach six feet. On the far right against the wall is *Fremontodendron californicum*, a plant best suited to this warm position where its spreading branches can be tied in and left to produce a fine crop of bright yellow saucer-like flowers throughout the summer.

Following page

Here at Flintham Hall there is a remarkable collection of pelargoniums in a greenhouse. Their colours range from palest sugar pink and misty lilac to the deeper hues of scarlet, crimson and pillar-box red. Some resemble the flesh of uncooked salmon, others are as white as a swan's back. There are double-flowered as well as single-flowered kinds, and some have leaves with a cream variegation while their neighbours have bronzy zonal markings. As long as geraniums are dead-headed fairly frequently and given adequate attention without too much fussing, a show like this will go on for many months. With some gentle heat to keep the house free of frost, many will carry the odd flowering stem throughout the coldest days of winter. This collection is threaded with pale blue lobelia and a few petunias, which with similar treatment will continue to give of their flowers for an almost equal length of time. Above the heads of these pelargoniums are ripening bunches of 'Black Hamburgh' grapes, which will be ready for the dessert bowl in early autumn.

Chatsworth

DERBYSHIRE

Our earliest view of Chatsworth is given in an engraving by the Dutchman Johannes Kip showing the late seventeenth-century parterre and extensive formal features marching boldly up the hillside. At that time a cascade was installed, with a Temple or cascade house being added later. In 1724 Daniel Defoe wrote 'Out of the mouths of beasts, pipes, urns, etc., a whole river descends the slope of a hill a quarter of a mile in length....' The 4th Duke of Devonshire hired 'Capability' Brown to remodel the parkland, during which task he destroyed much of the earlier layout. It was the 6th Duke who in the 1820s appointed Joseph (later Sir Joseph) Paxton as head gardener and it was this celebrated hero of English garden history who planted trees extensively, designed the Emperor Fountain and created huge rockeries. His most famous contribution to Chatsworth was the Great Stove or Conservatory which he designed in association with Decimus Burton, who went on to build the Palm House at Kew. At Chatsworth Paxton was the first man to grow to flowering stage the exotic water-lily *Victoria amazonica*, whose leaf structure inspired the strengthening design for the supporting ribs of its special house. Sadly Paxton and Burton's great structure has not survived, but Paxton has a lasting memorial at Chatsworth: the serried rank of 'glass cases' positioned against the 'Conservative Wall'. Here *Camellia reticulata* planted around 1850 still flourish. One of the latest additions to Chatsworth's historic garden is the serpentine avenue of beech planted by the present Duke and Duchess in 1953.

Sir Joseph Paxton's range of glasshouses on the Conservative Wall at Chatsworth. Camellias he planted there in about 1850 still survive.

Chatsworth

The Maze at Chatsworth sits on the site of the Great Conservatory, or Stove, which was built between 1836 and 1840. Constructed from over one thousand yews planted in 1962, the hedge Maze consists of six concentric circles set within a double row of yews planted in a square. There are many kinds of maze, and the example at Chatsworth has its origins in designs known in medieval times and earlier. Apart from their intellectual appeal, mazes have often been designed simply to offer the excitement of discovering their 'goal' or to admit visitors to a new part of the garden found only via that route. The centre may contain a piece of statuary or, as in this example, a silvery-leaved weeping pear, *Pyrus salicifolia* 'Pendula', which contrasts well with the dark yew.

Pages 96–7
The Canal Pond is 314 yards long and was dug in 1702. One hundred and forty years later, anticipating a visit from Tsar Nicholas, Emperor of Russia, the 6th Duke of Devonshire decided to install a fountain with a spout higher than the Tsar's at Peterhof, which the Duke had seen in 1826. Paxton mustered his full engineering skills and set about building an eight-acre reservoir 350 feet above the house to collect the necessary volume of water to generate the gravity-fed spout. The work was finished – with the jet capable of pushing a plume of water almost three hundred feet into the air. Alas, Tsar Nicholas's visit did not materialize, but the great engineering feat was named in his honour and the Emperor Fountain still plays on occasions.

Chatsworth

The Ring Pond at Chatsworth is situated at the north end of the long Serpentine Hedge which was planted as recently as 1953 by the present Duke and Duchess of Devonshire. This unusually shaped hedge (not visible in the picture) is inspired by the crinkle-crankle wall at Hopton Hall. In its relatively short life it has been a victim of crashing forest trees but no scars are noticeable today. Among the rocks in the Ring Pond there is a seventeenth-century lead duck from whose beak water sometimes gushes. Water-lilies are still flowering as the first October leaves begin to fall. The pond is surrounded by a high beech hedge and an inner circle of tightly clipped yews which appear to have gathered like inquisitive students hoping to learn some great truth from an unseen mentor. Beneath the still waters of the Ring Pond lies the feeder pipe for the Emperor Fountain. In summer, shade is given by the outstretched limb of a Spanish chestnut whose girth, at five feet above ground level, is almost eighteen feet.

York Gate

ADEL, YORKSHIRE

Before his early death in 1982 Robin Spencer compiled a tongue-in-cheek entry for the National Garden Scheme's 'Yellow Book' in which he summed up the parts of his garden: 'orchard with pool, arbour, miniature pinetum, dell with stream, Folly, nut walk, peony bed, iris borders, fern border, herb garden, summerhouse, alley, white and silver garden, two vegetable gardens and pavement maze', all contained within one acre! Photographs from that period reveal no hint of toy-town make-believe gardening, despite a description which might lead one to expect lurking gnomes. You are assured that none exist at York Gate. This is a masterly garden by any standards and one that most certainly must have been as much pleasure to construct and work in, as it is to visit. York Gate was acquired by Robin Spencer's parents in 1951, and his mother continues to maintain it to a standard which her son would, I feel sure, applaud. Mill stones set in gravel form the central path between two silver and white borders. The vista terminates between high hedges where a 'wobbly' barley-twist column surmounted by a stone ball converted to a sundial stands before open countryside. In the yew-enclosed herb garden another mill stone is set in gravel, and vertical emphasis comes from spiral-shaped box bushes rising from the mounds of fresh-green aromatics. At the end of the Iris Borders the summerhouse pulls the eye ever onwards to display Robin Spencer's cunning control of limited space.

A narrow view of the garden from the potting shed at York Gate. Rakes, hoes and brushes await their call.

York Gate

Here in the Herb Garden at York Gate the two borders of aromatic plants have been arranged each side of the gravel path. The area is enclosed by high walls of yew. Green-leaved and golden box plants have been clipped to form part of the permanent structure. A tall box spiral like the one shown here is the result of many years' patience and careful pruning, although pre-shaped forms in box (and indeed other evergreens) can now be purchased from garden centres and specialist nurseries – at a price. Both common sage (*Salvia officinalis*) and its purple form (*S. officialis* 'Purpurascens') are included in these borders together with rosemary – another evergreen surprisingly tolerant of very low temperatures.

Pages 104–5

The Iris Border will have been in full flower in early summer. Now, in July, only their foliage remains although a few poppies have infiltrated here and there. It is important to realize that with schemes involving only one group of plants the overall effect can be dazzling but brief. However, no one should be discouraged from making them. If the setting is strong – and here the brick criss-cross path makes a year-long satisfactory design – then that part of the garden will always give pleasure. Here at York Gate the Iris Borders are not isolated; when the flags have faded the eye is drawn to neighbouring features like the raised pool on the left where water-lilies and pond life can be observed at a comfortable height.

York Gate

Some all-white gardens have great appeal, and examples from around the temperate world crop up in numerous books; the finest, and certainly the best-known, is at Sissinghurst Castle in Kent, where Vita Sackville-West and Harold Nicolson began to garden in 1930. Earlier, Lawrence Johnston at Hidcote Manor in the Cotswolds made a white garden, which also survives to this day. There are many appropriate white-flowering plants to use in these schemes, and when bulbs are used, together with shrubs bearing pale, silvery leaves, it is possible to maintain a good-looking scheme all year round. But with summer's crowded hours white gardens reach their apogee. Included here are roses, astrantias, stachys, eucalyptus, veratrums, peonies, hostas, and the giant thistle, *Onopordum acanthium*.

Pages 108–9
Late afternoon shade at York Gate in July brings out the intense, glowing colours of herbaceous perennials. Spires of delphiniums and massed phloxes make good companions. A holly hedge and an upright golden yew stand in front of a raised canal pond, whose wall carries the espaliered limbs of the mighty blue cedar, *Cedrus atlantica glauca*, planted twenty-five years ago by Robin Spencer's mother. The 'arms' of the cedar now run approximately twenty feet either side of the main stem. Mrs Spencer copied this unusual feature from a local example which exists no more. The spring-fed pond collects great quantities of silt, which has to be removed from time to time, but one bonus granted by moving water is that it rarely freezes.

Holehird Gardens

TROUTBECK BRIDGE, CUMBRIA

The Holehird Gardens are home to the Lakeland Horticultural Society, which was founded in 1969. From part of the gardens there are dramatic, long-reaching views of Coniston Old Man, Allen Crags, and Scafell Pike which rises to over 3000 feet. The estate was bequeathed to Westmorland County Council by the late H. Leigh Groves at the end of the Second World War. Previously it had belonged to John Dunlop, the Manchester industrialist, who extended the mansion and added to the acreage. According to legend, its history goes back to the time of Edward VI who died at the age of sixteen in 1553. It was this young king who gave a parcel of land in Troutbeck Park as a holding to Hugh Hird, 'who so impressed the King with his feats of strength'. During the last thirty years of the nineteenth century John Dunlop made a large formal garden, terraces, tennis and croquet lawns, and the existing walled garden where, in Victorian days, there were vineries, peach house and fruit trees. When William Grimble Groves (H. Leigh Groves' father) acquired the estate, he, too, made further extensions to the mansion and built a range of glasshouses for his orchid collection. The range of glass was demolished eventually in 1974. William Groves was one of the sponsors of Reginal Farrer and William Purdom's plant-hunting expedition to China in 1914–15. Plants from that trip can still be seen in the garden, although most were lost during the 1940s when the last war robbed this and many other great gardens of their necessary labour force.

Sedums and sapphire-coloured gentians flowering in October among the heathers and fuchsias at Holehird Gardens in the Lake District.

Holehird Gardens

An October view over late-flowering mophead hydrangeas reveals the Lake District mountains of Wetherlam (2500 feet) and Crinkle Crags (2600 feet) ten miles away. A finger of Lake Windermere can be seen among the woods and fields. Rainfall records have been kept at Holehird since the beginning of the century. They show that over the past seventy years the average has been 69 inches a year, compared with a mere 20 inches recorded on the other side of the country around the Thames estuary. The mansion at Holehird Gardens is now leased as a nursing home to the charitable Leonard Cheshire Foundation, whose sick or disabled residents can enjoy the flowery and tranquil settings of a country garden.

Following page

A large, sloping bed is filled with acid-loving heathers and coniferous trees in all their autumn glory. Holehird encompasses a wide range of display beds and many ornamental trees. Among the more unusual specimens encountered on a long perambulating stroll are black mulberry (*Morus nigra*); the tulip tree (*Liriodendron tulipifera*), introduced to British gardens from North America at the end of the seventeenth century; the pocket-handkerchief or ghost tree (*Davidia involucrata*), with conspicuous white bracts that flutter in May breezes; *Magnolia obovata*, which, when a little older, will produce creamy, fragrant flowers 8 inches across; and *Juniperus recurva coxii*, discovered in Upper Burma by Euan Cox and Reginald Farrer in 1920. The former walled Kitchen Garden now has herbaceous borders and a good collection of climbing plants.

Levens Hall

NR KENDAL, CUMBRIA

Levens Hall is famous today for its topiary garden where yew and box have been clipped into geometric and random shapes, but there are many other interesting aspects to this late seventeenth- and early eighteenth-century garden. The park is partitioned from the garden by England's first ha-ha, built in 1695. A wide avenue of sycamores lines a grass ride, and a beech alley – underplanted with pungent wild garlic creating a green and white springtime carpet – is interrupted by a roundel with arches looking east and west. The garden was designed by M. Guillaume Beaumont, a Frenchman who lived at the time of the famous landscape architect, Le Nôtre, whose fantastically formal design ideas radiated from Versailles and Vaux-le-Vicomte. Levens has nothing of the grandeur of these French gardens; it is smaller, too. Here elegant pieces of topiary – tall and often unsymmetrically placed – stand about in grass. Other specimens rise from box-edged beds, where bulbs are succeeded by colourful annuals and some perennials in blocks of single colour. Typical of any one season's 'bedding' is a medley of *Verbena rigida*, richly hued wallflowers, sky-blue cynoglossum, or mats of cineraria, among whose silvery cut-leaved foliage stand dark red *Lobelia cardinalis*. The topiary itself, of green and golden yew as well as box, is a wonderful ragbag of assorted shapes and sizes: chessmen, spirals, mushrooms and umbrellas lend rhythm and movement to the more solid-looking cubes and pyramids. In the summer it seems as if flames lick the contours of the topiary as fiery-coloured flowers of invasive tropaeolum scroll and flutter over the pieces.

The Autumn digging of beds surrounding the topiary. The yellow Argyranthemum frutescens *'Jamaica Primrose' will flower on until the first frosts.*

Levens Hall

The beginnings of topiary are not known for sure; the Romans certainly cut trees and bushes into unlikely shapes. It was, however, hundreds of years later, in the seventeenth century, that topiary became widespread. Its true peak was reached in Renaissance gardens all over Europe. Besides Levens Hall there are famous topiary gardens at Hever Castle in Kent, Packwood House in Warwickshire, Rodmarton Manor in the Cotwolds, and Haseley Court in Oxfordshire, with numerous individual pieces adorning countless English gardens from grand castles to the humble cottage.

Previous page

Glimpses of colour can be seen in beds around the topiary. Yellow pansies in one, *Verbena rigida* in another, *Heuchera* 'Palace Purple' in the centre foreground. The two plants used for the topiary here are box (*Buxus sempervirens*) and yew (*Taxus baccata*). The shiny box leaves reflect light while the yews seem to absorb sunshine, creating shapes with a 'matt finish'. Golden yew is also used in the garden; in this picture there is the image of a crouching bird in the centre left. Other shapes appear to have grown randomly, as mushroom surmounts cone or tiered discs reach towards the sky. On the far right-hand side can be seen the leaves of *Ginkgo biloba*, the maidenhair tree, one of the few deciduous conifers, whose long-lived ancestors are native to eastern China.

122

The Priory

KEMERTON, WORCESTERSHIRE

The garden at The Priory is of a similar vintage to the Cokes' garden at Jenkyn Place in Hampshire. Although not far from the north-western boundary of the Cotswolds, this garden has Bredon Hill for its backdrop. When the Healings arrived at The Priory towards the end of the Second World War, they found a few trees and three existing herbaceous borders, which have since become the core of this remarkably colourful garden. Hedges were planted in the very early days and trees such as walnut, mulberry and maples were also started. Today, some forty-five years later, the garden seems happily mature, well-proportioned and, despite its riotous colour, delightfully restful. The trees have spread their limbs over thick yew hedges where buttresses of yet more clipped yew appear to strengthen the form. A wooden pergola has been draped in roses, clematis and vines, and the old walls of a ruined building, which may or may not have been a priory, have more roses pinned to their ancient stones. The three main borders are colour-graded though only one concerns itself strictly with one narrow band of pigment. The main border deals in shades of grey (foliage), white, cream and pale yellow (flowers), deepening to red and maroon before reversing Jekyll-like to paler hues. The second border, nearer the house, trades in pink and lavender among the whites and creams. The third, and smallest, is a masterpiece of garnet and ruby, scarlet and crimson, bronze and purple. In yet another area there is the 'hidden' June Garden where old roses scramble among soft-coloured perennials.

The white and grey end of a herbaceous border. Annual cosmos billows over artemisias next to sedums beloved by butterflies.

The Priory

The Red Border at The Priory is a masterpiece of colour-related planting using one section of the spectrum for the flowers and most of the foliage. Peter Healing has written of his Red Border: 'It would never become garish or too strong as there are so many really dark reds and bronze flowers and foliage to choose from and these would absorb the heat of the scarlets.' It might seem easy to make such a collection of reds from catalogues and gardening books but in reality it works very rarely. At its best for a few months from August on, this collection consists of *Rosa glauca*, ruby chard, 'Bishop of Llandaff' dahlias, penstemons, purple-leaved berberis, and 'black-faced' aeoniums, which need to be lifted before frost comes and stored away from the cold during winter.

Following page

This long herbaceous border was photographed in October and shows some perennial plants which have already run to seed but whose contribution to the scheme is still of value. On the far left there are white cosmos with a few white and pink dahlias among them. Below the adjacent Michaelmas daisies there is a clump of dark-leaved, deep violet-blue heliotrope. Yellow and brick-red rudbeckias fill in below the flat-topped yarrow, which very often gets through the summer without any need for staking. Deep-red dahlias and a clump of ruby chard hint at the theme which materializes so splendidly in its own Red Border nearby. Behind the yew hedge is the June Garden whose palette consists of much softer colours. This border can be expected to continue its performance until the first real frost knocks it to the ground.

Old Court Nurseries

COLWALL, WORCESTERSHIRE

Old Court Nurseries is situated on the outskirts of Colwall village at the foot of the Malverns Hills. It is famous today for its Michaelmas daisies which have been grown here since the time when Ernest Ballard, a friend of the author, publisher and gardener, William Robinson (1838–1935), owned the garden. Ernest Ballard raised 'Beauty of Colwall' here. It was the first *double* Michaelmas daisy, and it won the Royal Horticultural Society's First Class Certificate in 1907. Ernest Ballard was succeeded at Old Court by Percy Picton, one of William Robinson's gardeners at Gravetye Manor in Sussex, in 1951. Percy's son Paul now runs Old Court Nurseries with his wife Meriel. It has been called the home of Michaelmas daisies. Together they hold part of the National Collection of these asters and the best time to see them is in September and early October. In borders mixed with other late-flowering perennials like rudbeckias, heleniums, chrysanthemums and dahlias, Michaelmas daisies ensure a long succession of colour up to the first hard frosts. The two species which have given rise to most of the named varieties are *Aster novae-angliae* and *A. novi-belgii*. They prefer sun but are tolerant of partial shade, and the free-draining soil they demand must also ensure an element of constant moisture. Mildew can be a problem although there are several proven sprays to combat its onset. Michaelmas daisies can be increased by stem cuttings or by division. There are Michaelmas daisy varieties as short as a few inches; others reach three to four feet and will need some helpful stakes. Among the best Michaelmas daisies is *Aster X frikartii*, with soft blue flowers which bloom over a long period. It looks perfect next to the glowing reds of autumnal peony foliage.

A gravel path between borders exploding with a galaxy of Michaelmas daisies at Old Court Nurseries near the Malvern Hills.

Old Court Nurseries

In the Picton Garden at Old Court, Michaelmas daisies are grown on their own without any interference from other groups of plants. They can make a dazzling splash of colour in bright autumn sunshine or they can glow richly under dark thunderclouds when midday October light can appear like gloaming. There have been previous gardens devoted entirely to Michaelmas daisies. In 1899 Gertrude Jekyll wrote in *Wood and Garden*: '... it is a delightful surprise to pass through the pergola's last right-hand opening [at Munstead Wood, her Surrey home], and to come suddenly upon the Michaelmas Daisy garden in full beauty. Its clean, fresh, pure colouring, of pale and dark lilac, strong purple, and pure white, among masses of pale-green foliage, forms a contrast almost startling after the warm colouring of nearly everything else....'

Previous page

'White Wings' opposite the dark crimson-red 'Sophia' in the display beds at Old Court Nurseries. The colour range of these plants is enormous. Nurseries like this are important not only for their preservation and development of certain varieties but also for providing the opportunity to see exactly what you are buying. By comparing different varieties in a garden like this, you can choose the exact tone or hue for schemes of your own. Although Michaelmas daisies associate well with themselves, they are happy companions for a large range of late-flowering border plants. Here they can be seen with rudbeckias, heleniums, orange seed capsules of Chinese lanterns (*Physalis alkekengi*) and golden rod. Small button-flowered chrysanthemums will contribute their rich palette of colour within a few days.

Hever Castle

NR EDENBRIDGE, KENT

Hever Castle, built in the thirteenth century, belonged for a time to the Boleyn family, and it was here that Henry VIII courted Anne, who later became his second, and ill-fated, queen. The stone-built castle, in its two moats, then lapsed into comparative obscurity for several centuries until it was 'discovered' and bought by the American millionaire, William Waldorf Astor, in 1903. Astor lavished vast sums of money on the property, building a 'Tudor' village and making large formal gardens and a 35-acre lake. His architect was Frank Loughborough Pearson, who managed skilfully to build and restore the Castle in a thoroughly sympathetic manner. Pearson's contractor was the Sussex firm of Cheal & Sons of Crawley, and the appropriately named Messrs Cutbush supplied young topiary plants. Astor's fellow American, Edith Wharton, published her book on Italian villa gardens in 1904. In the same year William Waldorf Astor made his Italian garden, and it is furnished to this day with a collection of fine classical and Renaissance statuary from Italy which, although made to stand outside, is none the less protected through English winters. There are many elaborate features at Hever including a maze, a 'chess set' of topiaried yew, formal gardens, woodland and a long grassed drive or ride known as Anne Boleyn's Walk. William Waldorf Astor was not the first American to settle in England and make for himself an outstanding garden, nor was he the last, but Hever Castle stands as the supreme example of imported dollars rescuing a historic English house which, under different ownership today, can still be enjoyed by countless visitors.

The neatly clipped double row of chessmen at Hever Castle, 'carved' in yew, patiently awaits the first move.

Hever Castle

William Waldorf Astor was discerning as well as rich. He bought only the best statuary and he insisted upon first-rate workmanship. The results have proved long-lasting. It is almost ninety years since he began his restoration of Hever and his endeavours have proved to be a lasting investment. Here, November light falls upon the Castle walls. The deciduous trees have taken on their red and golden hues, and the creeper on the walls has a burnished glow. The garden is about to shut down for the winter but the crisp outlines of the topiary will ensure a bounty of elegant garden features which can be admired at any time of the year.

Following page

Hedge mazes appear in a number of English gardens. Apart from this and the one at Chatsworth – also photographed for this book – there are examples at Hampton Court near London, Glendurgan in Cornwall (made of laurel) and Longleat House in Wiltshire (the largest in the world). From this viewpoint it is possible to examine the structure of Hever's Maze and perhaps work out in advance of a visit exactly how to walk it. Beyond the Maze is one of two moats surrounding the castle, and to the left of the Maze, with a pergola separating them, is Anne Boleyn's Garden. In the far centre distance can be seen part of the five-acre Italian Garden where statuary and grottoes add to the authenticity of this period garden whose inspiration lies beyond the Alps.

The Grove

BRITWELL SALOME, OXFORDSHIRE

David Hicks is a designer whose romantic interiors are fashioned from exquisite fabrics and traditional furniture, fused together to create exciting but gracious rooms. In the garden he is concerned with form and foliage, relying on flowers mainly to bring perfume to his schemes. At The Grove, among Oxfordshire's undulating cornfields in sight of the Chiltern Hills, he has treated the land as an architect might treat his allotted building site. By making a series of outdoor rooms with walls and palisades of clipped chestnut and hornbeam he has built another house, albeit one without a roof. As all good designers know, space and the control of its effects are among the principal rules. David Hicks *has* space but he has distorted it with a number of 'framing' devices and by creating vistas which are not quite what they seem. One of his sleights of hand has been to 'extend' a grass ride which disappears in a swathe cut through a wood. Nearer the house, among the hedge-screened rooms, David Hicks has dug borders with Greek key patterns, made an enclosed rose garden where old and new varieties grow together among peonies and foxgloves, and constructed a 'tapestry' tunnel of native saplings intertwined with honeysuckles and clematis. The centre-piece of a raised terrace is a medallion of his mother-in-law, Countess Mountbatten of Burma, set into the wall of a rusticated stone niche. On the paving there are tubs of hydrangeas and tulips, and romping through the cracks are swatches of lavender and other aromatic plants which relish the warmth absorbed by the stone.

Gate piers topped by two canine statues guard the tennis court screened by a long run of 'American Pillar' roses.

The Grove

David Hicks has avoided the more usually encountered turquoise lining for his swimming pool. Seen from the dining-room terrace, this nonetheless welcoming sheet of water manages to achieve a more subtle impact. Surrounded by flat slabs and smooth river-stones it sits in its own lawn curtained by clipped chestnut trees. The vista has been made to appear longer than it really is by having a swathe cut through the fields to a wood where an avenue has been made as an extension of the grass ride. The rectangular pool is part of the geometry of the whole scheme, bringing the vista right to the house walls. This method of treating the landscape with a minimum of colour is typical of Mr Hicks's skill in making restful garden rooms.

Following page
This stone terrace at The Grove holds a medallion of David Hicks's mother-in-law, the late Countess Mountbatten of Burma. She is surrounded by a frame of sea shells and beach pebbles above a similarly framed lion's mask issuing water into a stone trough. The rusticated flint and stone arch is surmounted by a row of four ball finials, in line with the three steps leading from the garden level. Reaching above the top of the wall is a new folly with a castellated parapet built by David Hicks in 1990. Lilies, hostas, hydrangeas and roses are planted in terracotta pots, which stand about the terrace among clumps of lavender. During the summer months the terracotta pots need watering twice a day, and the hostas, particularly, must have their thirsts attended to conscientiously.

145

147

The Grove

This is David Hicks at his most restrained yet possibly most creative. The hedges are of clipped hornbeam on bare trunks with an inner row of the same trees set a little inside and stopped where the outer lines begin their bulk. The striped lawn is the result of careful mowing always in the same directions. Two large rectangles of grass have been allowed to grow to seeding stage, and among their tufts wild flowers have colonized. These rectangles will be clipped at the end of the growing season so that the whole area will look neat throughout the winter. The urns on pedestals have been niched into the corners of the hedges. The controlled mowing extends beyond the fencing, and gates beckon one to walk out into the large field of corn disappearing over the horizon. The dramatic arrowhead finials on the gate piers are made of plyboard and add a strong architectural embellishment. This remarkable use of space is also designed to be seen from the sitting-room window.

Chyverton

ZELAH, CORNWALL

Cornwall is renowed for its luxuriant gardens. The benign Gulf Stream brings mild breezes with plenty of moisture, although terrifying storms and occasional freeze-ups are the curse of the unsuspecting gardener. Chyverton is not among those fabled south-coast gardens hidden in a wooded valley beside an almost frost-free creek: it sits on the edge of Bodmin Moor, near the rugged north coast. The house was built for a Cornish mine owner, and the elegant, four-square Georgian building sits resplendent in two hundred acres of parkland developed between 1770 and 1825. Nigel Holman's parents bought the estate in 1924 and the garden we see today springs from a suggestion made by the great Cornish gardener J. C. Williams of Caerhays Castle, who recognized Chyverton's potential as a perfect woodland garden. During the Second World War the army occupied parts of Chyverton's land, and the economic climate of that time reduced the labour force to one. Magnolias planted before the war survived neglect, although many of the rhododendrons became infected with honey fungus. In 1953 Nigel Holman's father celebrated the Coronation of Queen Elizabeth II and his son's marriage to another Elisabeth by planting the Elis(z)abeth Glade whose first magnolias flowered fourteen years later in 1967. After his father's death in 1959 Nigel Holman took over the helm and in the past thirty years he has continued to expand the garden, introducing a number of newly discovered plants brought back as seed from horticultural and botanical expeditions. A stroll through Chyverton's woodland garden today presents a visitor with sumptuous acres of camellias, acers and rare trees and shrubs, as well as the many magnolias.

Massed camellias early in the year among sheltering trees at Chyverton.

Chyverton

The drive meanders through woods, over this stone bridge and across sloping parkland to the house. Yellow skunk cabbages, or bog arums (*Lysichiton americanus* – sometimes spelt *Lysichitum*), revel in the partial shade and boggy streamside soil. These quickly multiplying, deciduous perennials from the western states of America put up their bright sails of colour before the foliage develops. Their common name hints at their malodorous smell, which can carry for some distance. Long after the spathes have died down, the leaves – which can grow up to four feet high – will mask the edges to ponds and stream banks and look tidy until the first frosts. Lysichitums are long-lived and completely hardy in England and many parts of their native United States. At Chyverton these plants have colonized long runs of the shallow valley floor, where damp conditions prevail.

Sutton Park

SUTTON-ON-THE-FOREST, YORKSHIRE

The garden at Sutton Park dates only from 1963 although time was spent during the previous year ripping out laurels and other evergreens which were to play no part in the new scheme. The house is Georgian. Its formal façade of three storeys is flanked by two wings each terminating in idyllic pavilions built of the same brick. Mr and Mrs Sheffield invited their friend Percy Cane (1881–1976) to help design the beds on one of the terraces. Percy Cane made the gardens at Dartington Hall in Devon soon after the Second World War, and had also been commissioned to design gardens for the Emperor Haile Selassie's Imperial Palace at Addis Ababa. In the centre of Cane's terrace at Sutton Park he placed an old stone font-head depicting the twelve aspostles on its exterior. This noble piece of masonry, from Mr Sheffield's former Lincolnshire home, is planted in the summer with pelargoniums. The main terrace runs along the front of the house and is planted with flowers of a pale complexion: grey, pink and mauve. The terraces are 'retained' by a brick wall, from the centre of which wide steps lead onto stone paving running out to the Lily Canal. The house, framed by *Chamaecyparis lawsoniana* 'Allumii', is reflected in the still water. 'Capability' Brown worked on the parkland at Sutton Park and to this day tall trees planted years ago combine with those in a later-planted aboretum to form an important backdrop to the whole garden.

A striking use of several specimens of the weeping, silver, willow-leaved pear (Pyrus salicifolia 'Pendula') and a white, wirework gazebo.

Sutton Park

The formal, south, front of the house
showing the flights of steps leading from the
garden door to the terraces and the canal
with its bow-fronted protrusion. This
arrangement of house and garden is
exemplary; the formality of the design is
made to appear relaxed and restful by the
bountiful planting which tumbles over walls,
spills from stone urns, and runs among the
paving cracks on the higher steps. The silver,
almost white leaves of the weeping willow-
leaved pears contrast dramatically with the
dark evergreen trees which have been placed
to resemble the sort of columns to be found
around an open arena. Water-lilies prevent
the house's gracious façade being mirrored in
the summer months; during the winter and in
spring an inverted image of the house is
clearly seen on the still surface of the water.
The view is perfectly framed by mature trees
which are far enough away to be of no threat
to the building and yet seem to embrace and
protect it from the outside world. On days
when the air is still and the sky is this blue,
the house resembles a stage set awaiting the
performance of a uniquely English play in the
grand manner.

PHOTOGRAPHER'S NOTES

All the photographs in this book were taken on a Fuji G617 panoramic camera, which is equipped with a 105mm F8 lens and produces four exposures – each 6 × 17cm long – on a standard roll of 120 film. I used the new Fuji Velvia RVP transparency film throughout for its unrivalled brightness and ability to hold shadow detail. Although the camera has a basic viewfinder, I found that for framing accuracy I preferred to use a ground-glass screen attached to the camera back, but as with any plate camera, this meant that all compositions had to be made upside-down and back-to-front under the traditional black cloth (which frequently had a mind of its own in windy conditions).

While this long format is normally associated with wide panoramic vistas, I am just as interested in using its shape, so akin to the human field of vision, to record closer scenes. The selection and highlighting of small areas can be extremely effective in this format. All the usual rules about long exposures and small apertures have conspired against wanton flower heads (blowing in the inevitable breeze) remaining sharp, and many patient hours were required to capture some elusive scenes.

Thanks must go to David Wheeler for his inspired choice of unusual gardens suitable for the panoramic format. His immediate grasp of what I was trying to achieve made the whole project an inspiration and delight – despite the many long phone calls and constantly changing arrangements that had to be squeezed into our busy schedules. I could happily have spent hours in these glorious places even without a camera, and I would like to thank all the owners and gardeners who have so generously allowed me into their personal sanctuaries. I hope you will enjoy these private glimpses as a tribute to their forethought, imagination, enthusiasm and painstaking work over many years, which has continued a tradition and created a priceless legacy for the next generation.

Behind the scenes in the potting shed at Flintham Hall, Nottinghamshire.

INDEX

Page numbers in *italics* refer to photographs, those in **bold** to major sections, which include photographs.